Roman
INVADERS
AND SETTLERS

Barry M. Marsden

Wayland

Invaders and Settlers

Norman Invaders and Settlers

Roman Invaders and Settlers

Saxon Invaders and Settlers

Viking Invaders and Settlers

Series Editor: James Kerr

Designer: Loraine Hayes

Consultant: Mark Gardiner BA FSA MIFA Deputy Director, Field Archaeology Unit (Institute of Archaeology, London).

This edition published in 1994 by Wayland (Publishers) Limited

First published in 1992 by Wayland (Publishers) Limited, 61 Western Road, Hove, East Sussex, BN3 1JD

British Library Cataloguing in Publication Data
Marsden, Barry M.
    Roman Invaders and Settlers. –
    I. Title
    936

ISBN 0-7502-1355-8

Typeset by Dorchester Typesetting Group Limited
Printed and bound in Italy by Rotolito Lombarda S.p.A., Milan

Cover pictures:
Extreme top: Carved face of the god Sul.
Left: A Roman lighthouse.
Top middle: Reconstruction of a kitchen in a Roman villa.
Top right: Remains of a Roman leather shoe.
Bottom middle: Motif of the twentieth legion of the Roman army.
Bottom right: Main stages in the Roman conquest of Britain.
Back: Roman mosaic of the goddess Flora.

Pictures opposite:
Top: Roman medical instrument.
Middle: A swimming pool at Roman baths.
Bottom: A hypocaust system.

CONTENTS

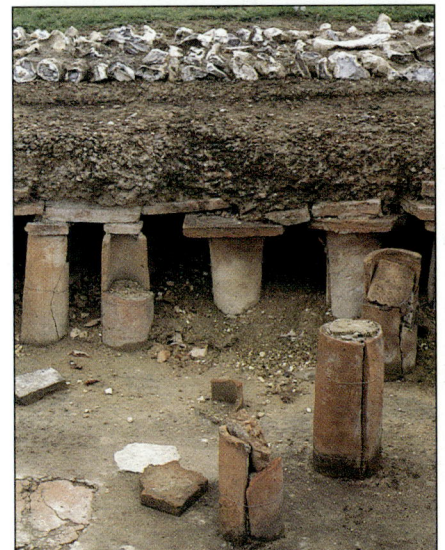

All words that appear in **bold** in the text are defined in the glossary.

Late Celtic Britain

By the late Iron Age much of Britain was divided into tribal kingdoms ruled over by chieftains. Their settlements were protected by hill-forts, which were surrounded by deep ditches and high earth **ramparts** topped with wooden fences. The entrances were carefully designed to make attacks very difficult.

Tribal territories of the Belgae in late Iron Age and early Roman Britain.

Though many of these forts were on higher ground, some were built on low-lying land. Maiden Castle in Dorset is a good example of a well-preserved Iron Age hill-fort. Around the hill-forts was farmland where most of the tribespeople lived and worked.

After 100 BC groups of people from Europe known as the Belgae moved into south-east England. The war-like Belgae speedily conquered the tribes to the north and west and created powerful kingdoms in the land they had seized. They used light war **chariots**, and were skilled metal workers who produced splendid weapons and ornaments. Though they had no written language they introduced new things like coins, copied from Greek ones, and the potter's wheel. Their priests were the Druids, a powerful group of people who carried out human sacrifices as part of their religion.

The Belgae in Britain traded with the Roman world, especially after the Roman conquest of **Gaul**. A wide range of Roman goods was transported to the big markets at the tribal capitals of Colchester and St. Albans, including pottery, trinkets and wine. Roman writers tell us that Britain was famous for its corn, slaves, hides and hunting dogs, which were traded to the Roman merchants. The Belgae cremated (burnt) their dead, and the extent of their trade with Rome can be seen in grave-goods. These often included pots and other articles that Roman traders had brought to Britain.

These large storage jars, called amphorae, *held wine, olives or sauces. They were brought to Britain from Rome by ship.*

The Roman army

The Roman army was made up of legions; highly-trained and heavily-armed foot soldiers who had to be Romans, not foreigners or slaves. Each legion had some 5500 fighting troops who used similar armour and weapons. We can see the type of equipment they used on carvings on tombstones and by the discovery of actual pieces of armour from places where the soldiers were based, such as forts and supply bases.

At the time the Romans invaded Britain, a typical soldier was dressed like the one in the picture, with a bronze helmet, a breastplate of metal strips over leather fastened with laces and buckles, a kilt (skirt) made from heavy cloth and thick-soled hobnailed leather sandals.

His weapons included a short stabbing sword (*gladius*), a dagger, a throwing spear (*pilum*) or two, and a curved oblong shield. Legions had their own **artillery**, transport, builders and medical staff. During campaigns they built their own defences (marching camps) whilst in hostile territory. They lived in permanent forts when they were on **garrison** duty.

Auxiliary regiments fought alongside the legions. These regiments were not made up of Romans, but of people who came from countries Rome had conquered, and they only served in foreign lands. Their forces were divided into groups of 500 or 1000 soldiers. They often fought with the sort of weapons – such as bows or slings – that were used in their own countries, as well as with Roman swords and shields. The auxiliaries had cavalry units which could scout for the legions, or chase defeated enemies.

The auxiliaries and the legionaries served in the army for twenty-five years. On retirement, a legionary was given land and a pension while an auxiliary was given Roman citizenship.

RIGHT *Roman legionaries and layout of a fort.* LEFT *Medical staff attached to the legions would have had a medical kit like this.*

Invasion and conquest

In 55 BC and 54 BC Julius Caesar led expeditions to south-east England. Though he defeated the local tribes, he only stayed a short while and there was no permanent conquest. However, in AD 43 Emperor Claudius ordered an invasion, firstly to impress his subjects but also to take some of the wealth which Britain possessed, especially in corn and valuable metals such as iron. Four legions, the second, ninth, fourteenth and twentieth, with auxiliaries, landed in Kent and by AD 47 had conquered the south of England and part of the Midlands. In the south-west the second legion stormed many hill-forts, including Maiden Castle, where archaeologists discovered a war cemetery of Britons killed in the battle. In the spine of one skeleton was a large iron arrowhead, which was shot from a *ballista*, a huge crossbow used to bombard enemies.

A roof tile from Chester decorated with the boar of the twentieth legion.

In AD 60 the queen of the Iceni tribe, Boudicca, led a rebellion against the Romans. Boudicca was protesting against the heavy taxes the Romans demanded, and the harsh treatment she and her family received from Roman agents. They wanted the riches Boudicca's dead husband Prasutagus had left to the Emperor in his will. Her forces destroyed the Roman settlements at Colchester, London and St. Albans, and killed all the inhabitants. They also wiped out a Roman force sent from Lincoln to stop them. Boudicca's army was finally defeated by the Governor Paullinus, and all hope that the Romans would be driven out of Britain was lost.

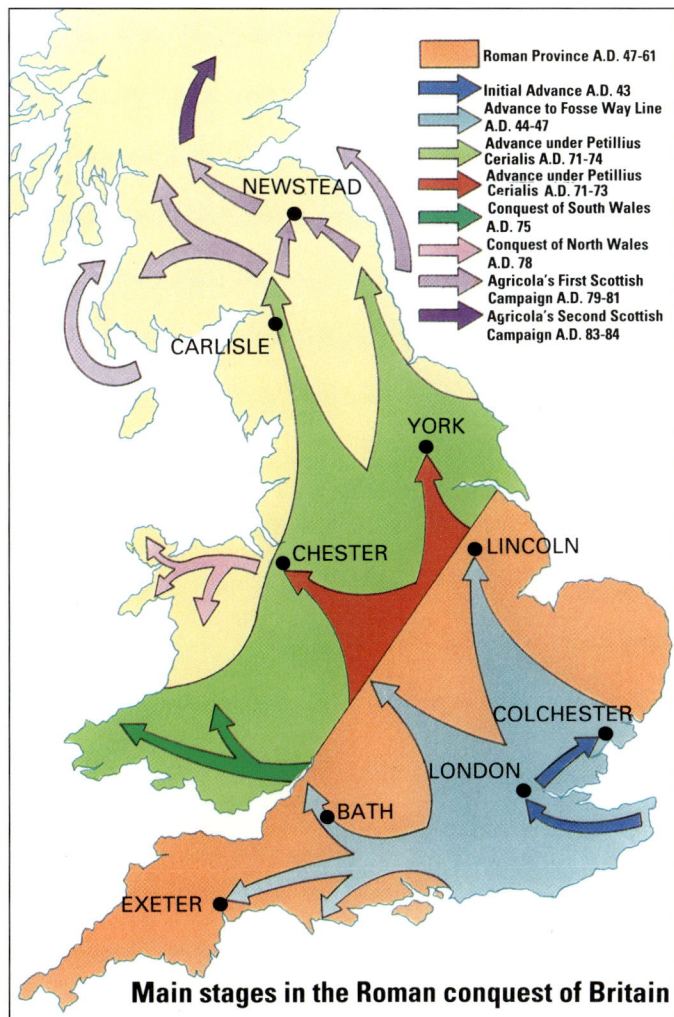

Major roads and towns of Roman Britain

HADRIAN'S WALL

ALDBOROUGH
YORK
CHESTER
LINCOLN
WROXETER
LEICESTER
COLCHESTER
GLOUCESTER
ST. ALBANS
CIRENCESTER
BATH
SILCHESTER
LONDON

— Major roads

	Roman Province A.D. 47-61
	Initial Advance A.D. 43
	Advance to Fosse Way Line A.D. 44-47
	Advance under Petillius Cerialis A.D. 71-74
	Advance under Petillius Cerialis A.D. 71-73
	Conquest of South Wales A.D. 75
	Conquest of North Wales A.D. 78
	Agricola's First Scottish Campaign A.D. 79-81
	Agricola's Second Scottish Campaign A.D. 83-84

NEWSTEAD
CARLISLE
YORK
CHESTER
LINCOLN
COLCHESTER
LONDON
BATH
EXETER

Main stages in the Roman conquest of Britain

In the AD 70s, the Romans occupied the territory of the Brigantes in northern England, which had previously been ruled by their **ally** Queen Cartimandua, and they also took control of Wales. Between AD 81 and 84 the famous general Agricola defeated the war-like Pictish tribes of Scotland and most of Britain came under Roman control. However, as time went on the Romans could not spare the large number of troops needed to keep control of the whole country. In the early second century AD the Picts regained the north, driving the Romans back into Brigantia.

Roman Games

To keep their territory peaceful the Romans built auxiliary forts at vital points, and garrisoned them with 300-500 auxiliaries. At Corbridge, near Hadrian's Wall, traces of games played by the off-duty soldiers were found. One of these games was called *ludus latrunculorum* (a *latro* was a kind of soldier) and you can make your own example of this game.

WHAT YOU NEED: self-hardening clay, thick cardboard, scissors, paint, felt-tipped pen.

WHAT TO DO:
1. Roll out the clay and make it into twenty-four round flat counters about 1 cm across and 2 mm thick. If you wish you can colour them with paint when the clay is dry. Use two colours, one for each set of twelve counters.
2. Next cut out a thick piece of cardboard 16 cm square.
3. Using a felt-tipped pen divide this board into eight rows of eight squares, each 2 cm square.

The game can be played like modern draughts. The idea is to capture an 'enemy' piece by trapping it between two of your own.

Frontiers

The Emperor Hadrian came to Britain in AD 122 and ordered the building of a wall from east to west, from the River Tyne to Solway Firth. It was built to separate the Brigantes from the tribes of southern Scotland and to keep them from joining their forces together. This wall was nearly 120 km long, 6 m high and up to 3 m thick. Two-thirds of the wall was built in stone, but the final western section was first made of earth with wooden buildings and then later replaced with stone.

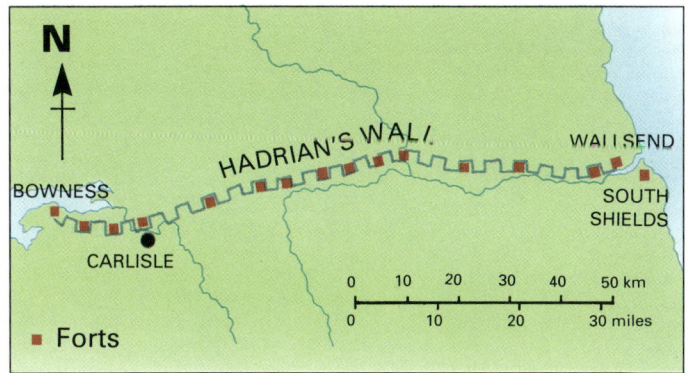

At every Roman mile (about 1500 m) was a small fort called a **milecastle**, and between each milecastle were two signalling turrets. Sixteen forts were added to the defences when they were almost complete.

This milestone stands in its original place on a road near the fort at Vindolanda.

*The **lavatory** block at Housesteads fort on Hadrian's Wall.*

A deep ditch was dug in front of the wall. Behind the wall was a supply road and behind this a flat-bottomed ditch with a mound on either side, called the *vallum*. Hadrian's Wall marked the northern frontier of Roman Britain.

The remains of many of the forts can still be seen, including Housesteads (Vercovicium) and Chesters (Cilurnum). The buildings of these forts have all been **excavated**, and include the military headquarters, the commander's house, **granaries** and barracks. Housesteads has a well-preserved lavatory block and Chesters has a fine bath house outside the walls. Many forts attracted traders and shopkeepers, and a small town called a *vicus* often grew up next to one of the fort's gates. Soldiers' wives and families lived there, and a carefully excavated *vicus* can be seen at Vindolanda, near Hadrian's Wall, together with reconstructed sections of both the stone and the turf wall.

In AD 140 Hadrian's Wall was abandoned, because a turf wall was built further north in Scotland between the Clyde and the Forth. This wall had a ditch in front, and all the forts were made of wood. Although only half the length of Hadrian's Wall, and needing a much smaller garrison to guard it, the Antonine Wall was not a success, and within a short time it was completely abandoned. Hadrian's Wall again became the northern frontier and was used almost until the time the Roman troops left Britain.

There were probably around one million people living in Roman Britain. Possibly one hundred thousand of these came from the Roman empire and about half of these were soldiers. The others included officials, merchants and craft-workers. The Romans encouraged the British tribes to run their own local affairs, and their leaders were easily persuaded to adopt a Roman way of life. Most of the Roman **civilians** who came to Britain lived in the larger towns such as London and York. We call these people, and the Britons who adopted Roman customs and life, Romano-British.

A mosaic from Cirencester which shows Flora (the goddess of spring) with flowers and a bird on her shoulder.

Model of a section of Hadrian's Wall

WHAT YOU NEED: baseboard, self-hardening clay or coloured plasticine.

WHAT TO DO:

1. Place a thin layer of clay or green plasticine about 0.5 cm thick over the baseboard, and cut out the frontier ditch which should be 'V' shaped.

2. Behind the ditch build up the line of the wall in clay or white plasticine (about 1.5 cm high and 0.5 cm thick).

This picture shows how the fort of Chesters on Hadrian's Wall may have looked.

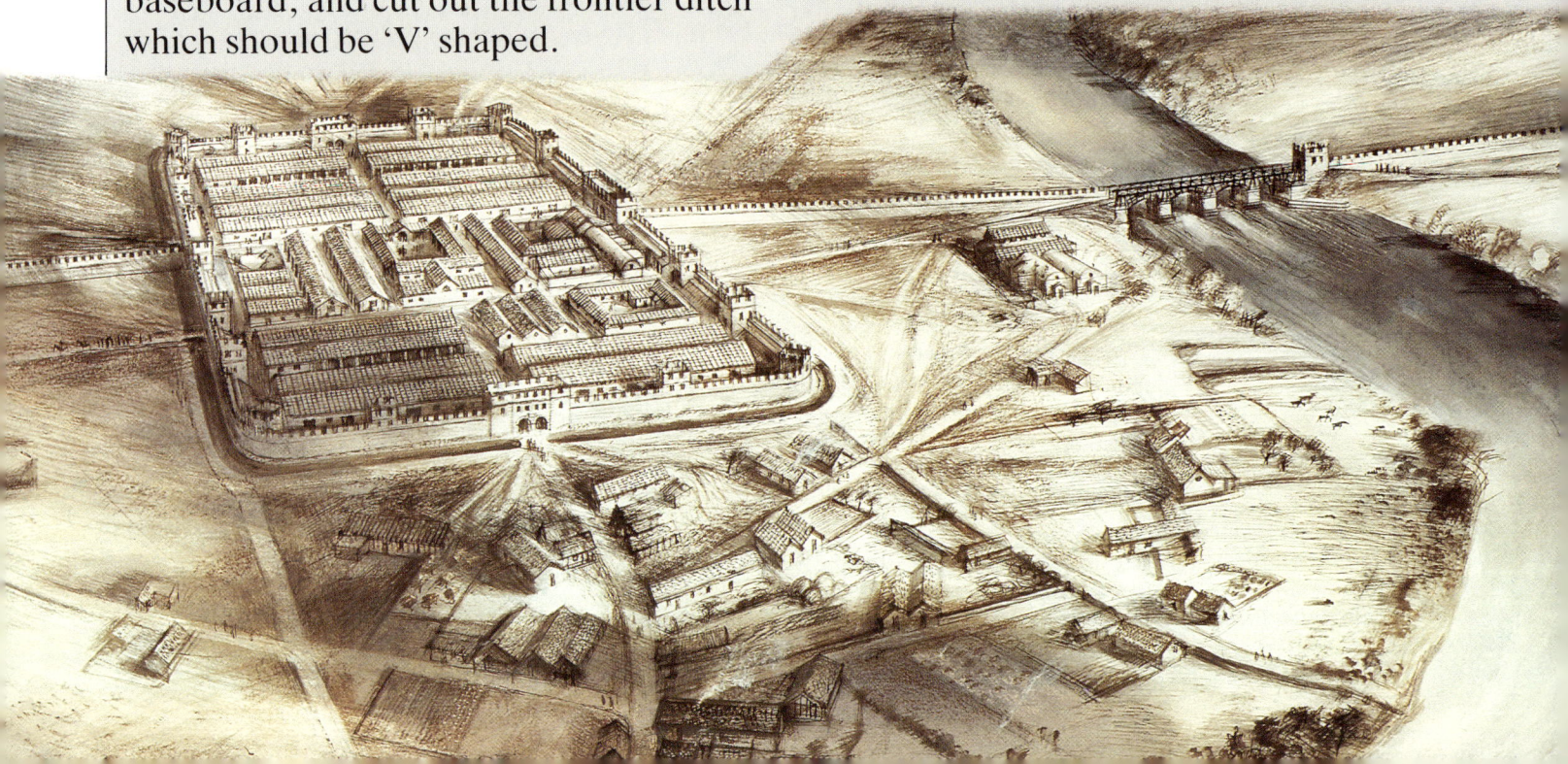

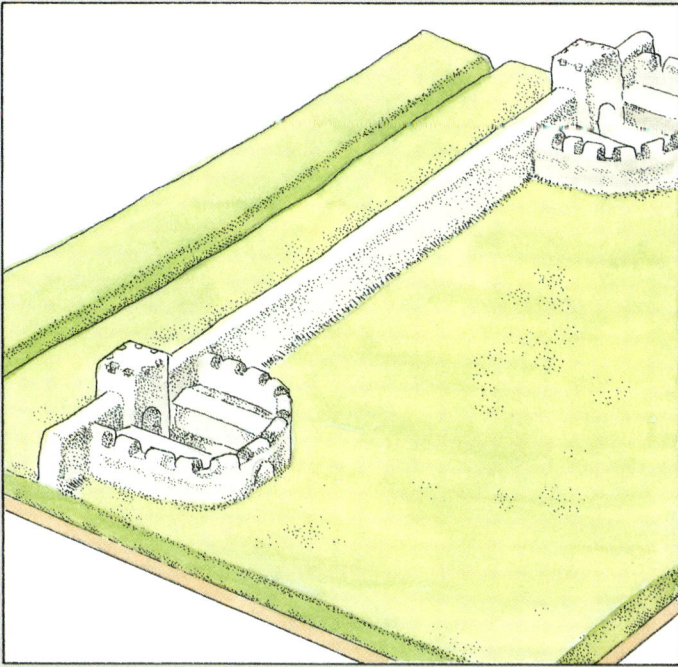

3. Place one milecastle near each end of the baseboard, and build them into the wall, checking their shape with the picture above. Each has a barrack block on either side of the main gate.

4. Two signalling turrets made from square blocks of plasticine can be placed between the milecastles.

5. Behind the wall a thin strip of brown plasticine laid on the green will represent the east-west supply road.

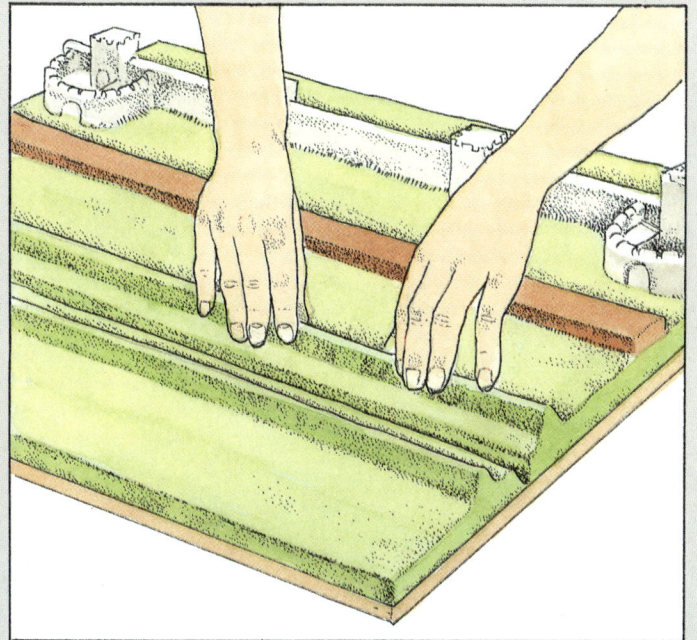

6. Some way behind this the line of the *vallum* can be cut out. Remember this was flat-bottomed. A thin strip of plasticine running along each side of the *vallum* will represent the banks of soil dug from the ditch.

Towns and town life

Towns, built mainly from the second century onwards, were a new idea for Britain and were laid out near the main tribal settlements. The costs of their upkeep were paid for by the surrounding country areas.

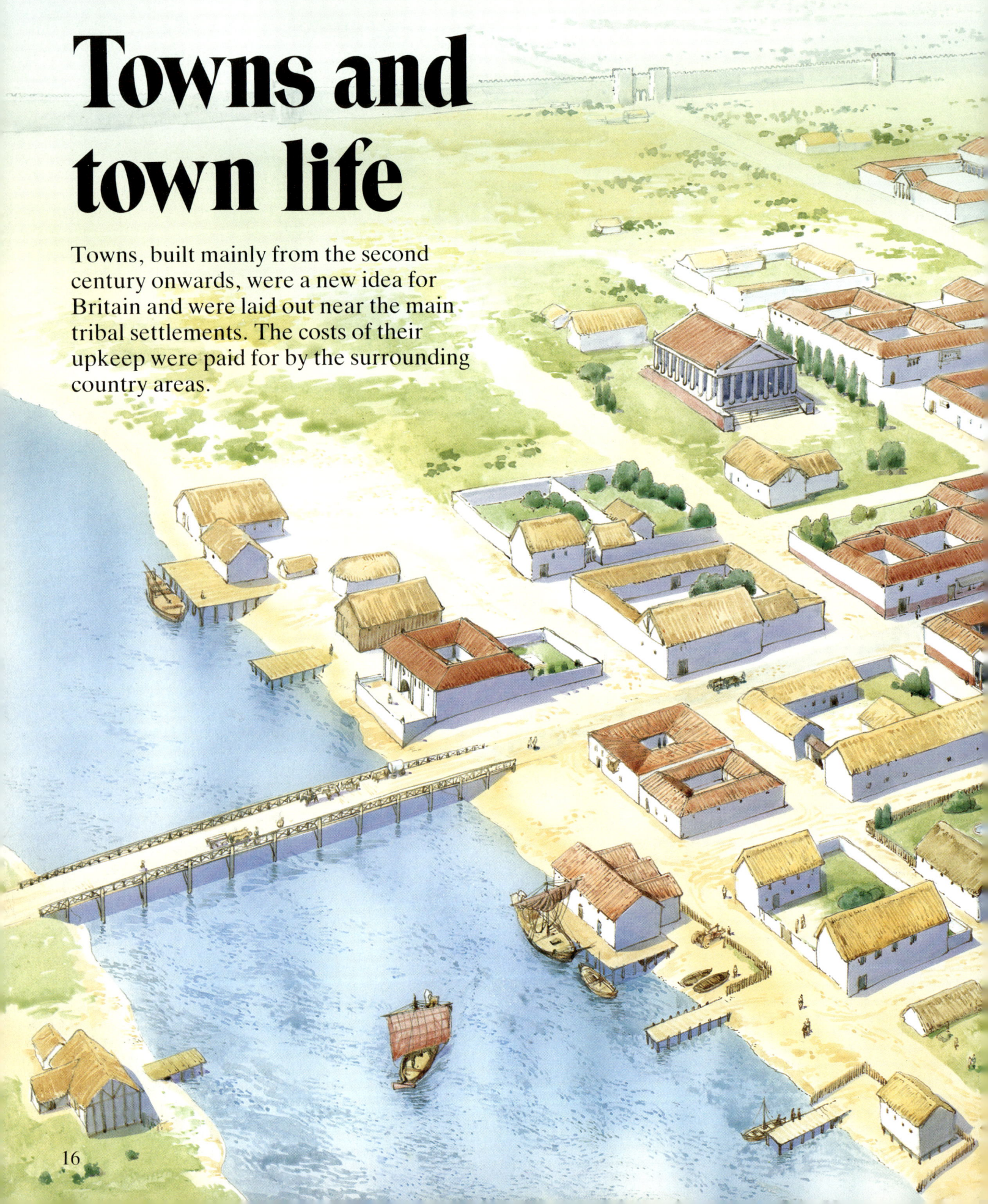

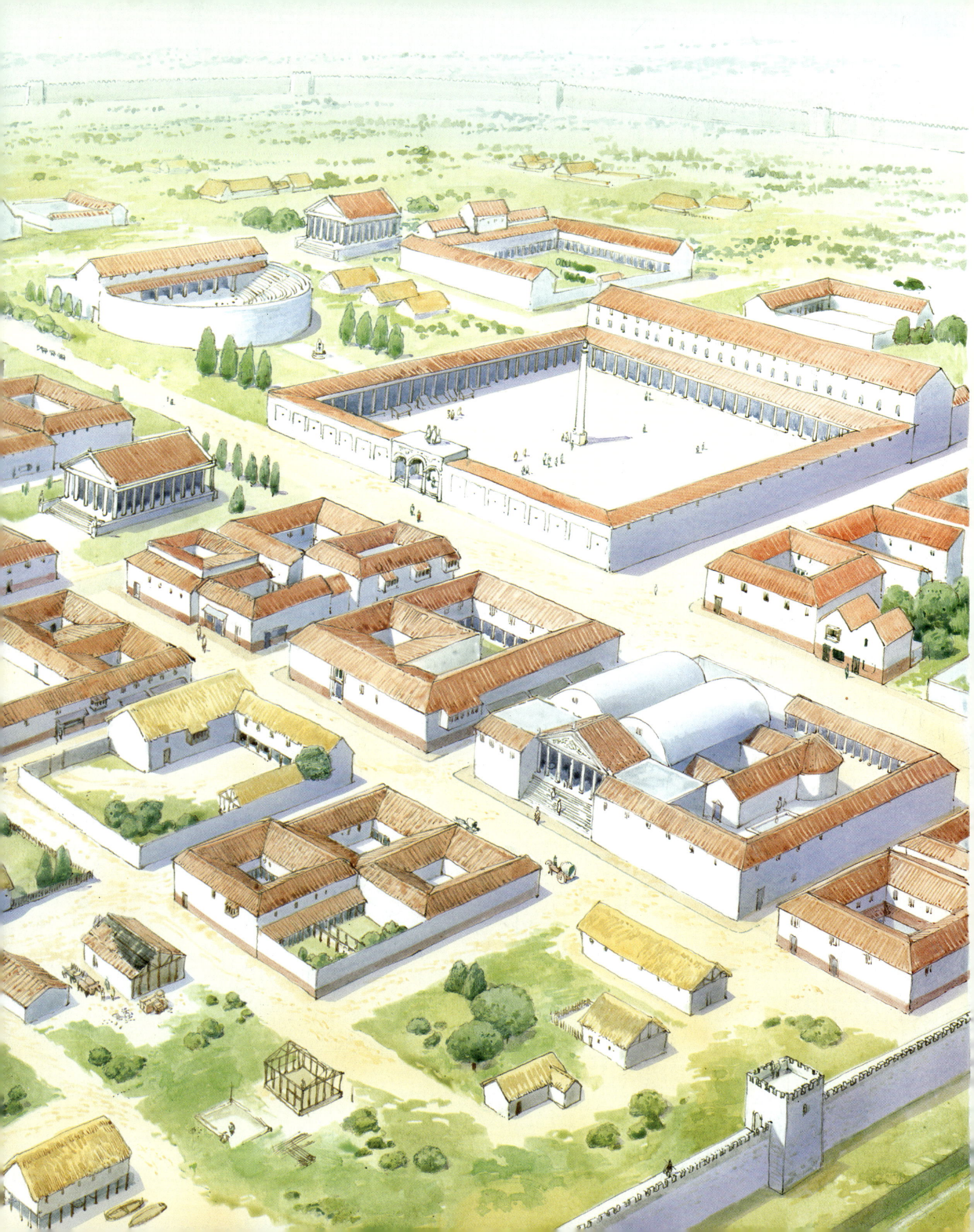

Tombstone of Regina, a merchant's wife.

BASILICA. The basilica, joined on to the forum, was the town hall where rates and taxes were paid and where local laws were passed.

AMPHITHEATRE. The **amphitheatre** was usually built outside the town walls, and was a place for popular entertainment. This could include bear-baiting, gladiator fights or circus acts of various types. A fine amphitheatre can be seen at Caerleon in South Wales.

WALLS and DITCHES. Ditches were dug to mark out the size of the town, but walls were only added when it became necessary to protect the people in times of unrest. Towns were divided into blocks, called **insulae**, by straight rows of streets.

FORUM. This was the market place where stalls and businesses were situated. It was also a central place where the townspeople could meet.

GATES. Most towns had large gates with big towers even though the surrounding walls were not built until the third century AD. One of the finest was the Balkerne Gate at Colchester.

CEMETERIES. By law the dead had to be buried outside the town walls, so cemeteries were laid out along the roads going into the town. The monuments included tombstones and **mausoleums** where offerings were made by families. Several large cemeteries have been found in York.

TOWN HOUSES. The Romans liked the chief tribal families to live in the towns, where they could see to the collection of taxes and make sure that local laws were obeyed. They lived in luxurious homes based on Roman models.

A Roman fortified tower.

TEMPLES. Many gods were worshipped by the Romans, and each town would have three or four small temples. Mithras was a popular god, and a fine temple to him was discovered in London in the 1950s.

An altar in honour of the god Jupiter.

The swimming pool at Bath.

BATHS. These were for the whole town to use, and many were large and luxurious (like the one at Wroxeter). They were meeting places where food and drinks were served, and had rooms for physical exercise. Most of the staff were slaves. Water was piped in through **conduits**.

MANSIO. This was a hostel where travellers could stay overnight. Rooms were simple and people cooked their own food in the kitchen provided.

Roman place names

Towns with *porta* (gate) and *castra* (fort) in their names were places where the Romans settled: for example Portsmouth and Doncaster. See how many Roman names you can pick out on a map of Britain.

Roman writing tablets

Two kinds of Roman writing tablets have been found in Britain. The commonest is the wax tablet. You can make your own writing tablet.

WHAT YOU NEED: thick cardboard, yellow plasticine, scissors.

WHAT TO DO:

1. Cut out a baseboard from the cardboard about 15 cm by 12 cm.
2. Gently press a block of yellow plasticine (the colour of the original beeswax) 0.5 cm thick on top of this.
3. Use a thin knitting needle to write messages on the flat surface of the plasticine.
4. Pass your message on to someone else; they can read it, smooth over the surface as the Romans did, and write their reply to you. The Romans often used two blocks of wax, and fastened them together with ribbon.

In the 1970s the first example of a completely different type of writing tablet was discovered at Vindolanda. You can make a copy of this writing tablet in the following way:

WHAT YOU NEED: four small strips of thin wood or stiff card, pen and ink, scissors, thin ribbons.

WHAT TO DO:
1. The strips of thin wood or card should be cut into pieces 15 cm by 6 cm.
2. Each piece should have two holes pierced in the same places along the short sides.
3. Using pen and ink, write a message

The Romans not only used writing tablets to pass on messages. A tile maker scratched this message on one of his tiles about a lazy workman called Augustalis.

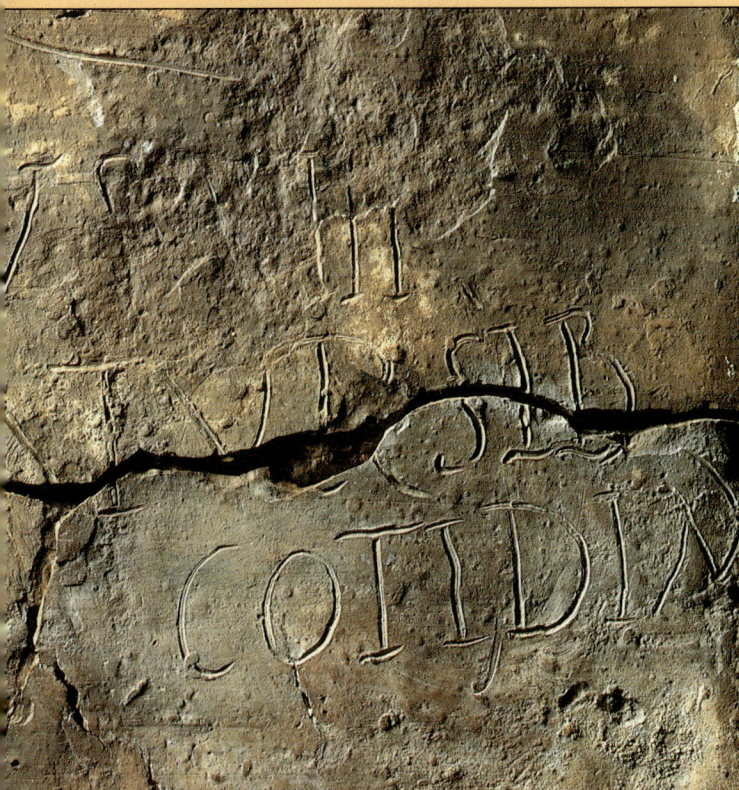

across the long sides of each 'page'.
4. The strips can then be joined to one another, using the ribbons and tie-holes.
5. Longer messages can be made using more strips, and the whole document can then be folded like a concertina.

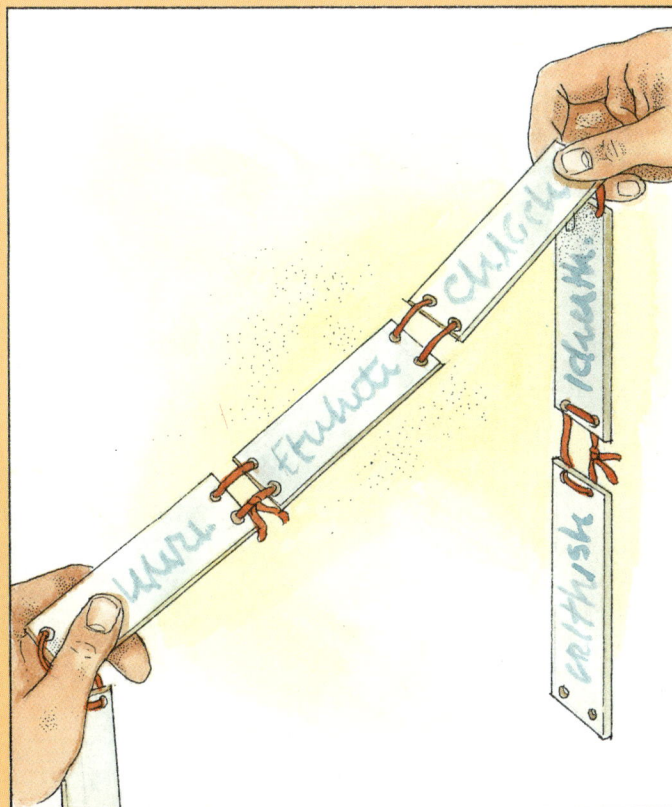

6. Unfold by holding the top sheet and pulling the bottom, and read the whole message across from left to right.

Villas

A villa was a country house lived in by a farmer or landowner. Many were built in Britain when town life became too expensive for tribal chieftains and they went back to live on their own lands.

Most villas probably started off as small houses with only a few rooms. The richer villa owners made a lot of money growing corn on a large scale using the labour of their own tribespeople whom they still ruled. With their profits they added extra rooms to each end of their houses, and sometimes knocked down and rebuilt their villas on a bigger scale.

Some of the largest villas, like Chedworth and Woodchester, had rooms grouped round a central courtyard. The bigger Roman households depended on slaves to do the work, both inside the house and on the land. The richer villa owners had fine painted plaster walls

A hypocaust system at a Roman villa in Hampshire.

and an underfloor heating system called a **hypocaust**. The floors of the rooms were laid with beautiful mosaics. Many villas had their own luxurious bathhouses and the owners bought expensive furniture and ornaments. However, while the well-off families lived in this way, the lives of the ordinary people of the tribes hardly changed. Most people continued to live in small villages in round huts with thatched roofs, and their way of life remained much as it had been before the conquest.

This is how the dining room of a villa would have looked.

Communications, trade and industry

Watling Street (RIGHT) *is a typically straight road originally built by the Romans. In Roman times, it would have looked like the one above.*

The Roman roads were built by the army to join the forts together and to allow legions to move swiftly from place to place. Later on, roads connected all the main towns. Many modern roads were laid on top of Roman ones like the Fosse Way and Watling Street. Milestones told travellers how far they were from their destinations (there is a picture of one near Vindolanda on page 11).

The roads were kept in good repair. Small towns often grew up at important places along the routes. Many trade goods were carried by boat on the canal systems dug by the Romans. Examples of these canals can be seen at Piercebridge in County Durham, the Car Dyke in Lincolnshire and the Raw Dykes in Leicester.

Goods came to Britain from all over the Roman Empire. They included large jars, called *amphorae*, for storing wine,

This lead bar was made at the Lutudarum lead works at Carsington in Derbyshire.

olives or sauces, fine red pottery from Gaul, ornaments and lamps from Italy and wine barrels from Germany. A reminder of the merchant ships that crossed the Channel can be seen in the grounds of Dover Castle, where a Roman lighthouse still stands. Under the influence of Roman rule many British potteries sprang up, producing fine jars, bowls and plates, from **kilns** in Northamptonshire, Derbyshire, Oxfordshire and the New Forest.

Many metals were mined, including gold from Dolocouthi in Wales. But the most valuable metal was lead which the Romans used for many purposes, especially water pipes. Lead was mined in Yorkshire and the Mendips. The most important area was the Derbyshire Peak, where a private company, based at Lutudarum (Carsington), mined the metal on behalf of the government. One of the biggest British products was grain and large amounts were grown on a vast scale on the villa farms to be **exported** to the rest of the empire.

Remains of the Roman lighthouse at Dover, which can be seen in the castle grounds.

Religion

The Romans, like the Britons, were pagans who worshipped many gods, including their emperors. One of the earliest Roman temples in Britain, to Emperor Claudius, was a splendid Greek-style building at Colchester; it was destroyed by Boudicca in AD 60. The Britons were allowed to keep their own gods, and these often became linked with Roman ones. At Bath the Celtic god Sul was joined with the goddess Minerva and they were both worshipped in a grand temple. Another Celtic god, Taranis, was linked with Jupiter and a temple at Wanborough in Surrey was raised to him.

Soldiers worshipped in this tiny temple.

Temples to many other gods have been found in Britain. The Egyptian goddess Serapis was worshipped in York, and the Persian god Mithras was very popular; temples to him have been found as far apart as Carrawburgh on Hadrian's Wall, Colchester and London. An excellent life-size reconstruction of the Carrawburgh site can be seen at the University of Newcastle Museum. Near this temple was a well dedicated to a local goddess, Coventina. When it was excavated, thousands of coins which had been thrown in as gifts by travellers were discovered. Other coin **hoards** have been found at temple sites at Bath and Buxton. Temples varied in style and size, but a typical one would be square in shape and surrounded by a covered veranda, and would measure around 15 m square.

Christianity was forbidden by Roman law until the fourth century, as it was seen as a threat to the rule of the emperors. Until then Christians were treated with great cruelty. When the government allowed them to worship openly, small churches were built in many places in Britain. An early Christian church has been found at Silchester.

The face of the Celtic god Sul.

Food and clothing

Clothing from Roman times has not survived in Britain so we have to look at statues and tombstones which often have carvings on them. These include both soldiers and civilians, and show the hairstyles as well as the clothing. Most men and women wore tunics which reached to their knees, with short or long sleeves. They also wore cloaks of varying length, fastened at the shoulder with a bronze brooch. Some of these cloaks were hooded. Very few men wore the **toga**, which was perhaps only for special occasions.

The museums at York and Chester have fine collections of tombstones which show the male and female fashions well. There was of course a difference between the clothes of richer people who could afford the best quality cloth and the poor who had to make do with cheaper and rougher fabrics.

A well-preserved Roman shoe and sandal. The shoe still has hobnails in the sole.

The kitchen of a villa, showing the storage jars and stove.

Some material, such as leather, survives well in damp conditions. Leather sandals, boots and other finds, including wooden objects such as writing tablets, have been found at several Roman settlements. Damp soil also preserves the remains of food such as bones, seeds and pips. Careful study of these finds shows us that the main diet of the Romano-Britons included beef, chicken, venison, small birds and fish, oysters and other shellfish. The food was cooked with herbs and strong sauces were used to add flavour. Vegetables, eggs and fruit were also eaten, and were washed down with beer and wine. Archaeologists have also found many of the cooking pots and pans used in the preparation of food. These include mixing bowls called **mortaria**, and small bronze pans and ladles.

Roman Custard

WHAT YOU NEED:
400 ml milk
50 ml clear honey
3 egg yolks
$1/4$ tsp nutmeg

WHAT TO DO:
You will need the help of an adult to make this dish.
1. Pour the milk into a bowl and mix with the honey.
2. Whisk the egg yolks in a separate bowl.
3. Pour the milk mixture into a saucepan and heat briefly.
4. Take it off the heat and add the well-beaten egg yolks. Add the nutmeg and stir thoroughly.
5. Pour into a baking dish and bake in a pre-heated oven at 165°C (325°F). It should set within an hour.

The end of Roman Britain

These massive bastions once defended the walls of the Saxon Shore fort at Pevensey.

During the third century AD the Roman world came under attack from **Barbarian** tribes living to the north of the Rhine and Danube frontiers. These tribes were able to invade because greedy Roman generals withdrew their legions from the frontier to fight each other in struggles to rule the empire. South-eastern England was attacked by Saxon pirates from north Germany and Holland. The Romans built a number of large fortresses from the Wash to the Isle of Wight to defend the coastline which was called the 'Saxon Shore'. The best remaining examples of these fortresses are those at Portchester, Hampshire, and Pevensey in Sussex. Some of these may date from the time of Carausius, a disgraced naval officer who proclaimed himself Emperor of Britain and ruled it in defiance of Rome from AD 286 until AD 293.

After AD 300 the Picts again became troublesome, and raiders from Ireland attacked the western coasts of Britain. In AD 367 these tribes joined forces in a mass invasion, aided by the Saxons, and the Emperor Valentinian had to send an army to rescue the Britons. By this time the legions had lost much of the strength and discipline they were famous for because they had allowed non-Romans into their ranks. In the AD 370s Count Theodosius built a line of signal stations along the east Yorkshire coast to give early warning of Saxon attacks; a good example can be seen in the grounds of Scarborough Castle.

Then in AD 383 a large part of the Roman army left Britain to fight in Gaul against the Barbarians and Hadrian's Wall was finally abandoned. The Yorkshire signal stations were destroyed in the AD 390s and the last Roman troops were withdrawn in AD 407 to defend Italy

Saxon shore forts

BRANCASTER

BURGH CASTLE

BRADWELL

RECULVER

RICHBOROUGH

LYMPNE   DOVER

PORTCHESTER   PEVENSEY

■ Saxon shore forts

A Yorkshire signal station.

from the **Germanic** invaders. By AD 410 Rome no longer ruled Britain and the Britons were left to defend themselves. No one believed at the time that this was the end of Roman rule, yet the Romans never returned, and some forty years later the Anglo-Saxons began settling permanently.

The Roman way of life lingered on for some time after the departure of the last soldiers, and towns and villas in the south-west of England were still lived in until the early sixth century. In most other areas the towns eventually became **derelict** and the villas crumbled. The roads were still used however, and many modern roads follow the line of earlier Roman ones. Christianity too lingered on and was revived by Celtic and Roman monks in the seventh century. Much of

the other evidence of Roman civilization – place names, language, art and architecture – was lost under the new invaders and settlers and was only rescued centuries later by the patient work of archaeologists and historians.

BC **AD**	**55 BC** Julius Caesar's first expedition to Britain. **54 BC** Caesar's second expedition.
	AD43 Invasion of southern Britain by Emperor Claudius' army. **60** Queen Boudicca led a rebellion against Roman rule. **71-74** Roman conquest of Brigantia. **75-78** Roman conquest of Wales. **81-84** The occupation of Scotland completed by Governor Agricola.
AD 100	**122** Emperor Hadrian visited the province and ordered the building of a wall from the Tyne to Solway. **140** The Antonine Wall built by Governor Urbicus, from the Forth to the Clyde. **197** Hadrian's Wall taken by the Picts, but later recaptured by the Romans.
AD 200	
AD 300	**286-293** Carausius ruled Britain.
AD 400	**367** Britain invaded and plundered by Picts, Scots and Saxons, who were finally driven out by Count Theodosius. **383** Large part of Roman army left Britain for Gaul. **407** Last Roman troops departed from Britain. **410** Britain ceased to be a province of Rome.

Glossary

Ally A country or ruler friendly with another country or ruler.

Amphitheatre An oval or round-shaped, open-air building with a central space surrounded by seating, where entertainments took place.

Artillery The heavier weapons of war such as the *ballista*.

Barbarian A member of the tribes who fought the Romans.

Chariots Light two-wheeled carts pulled by two horses used by the British tribes in warfare.

Civilians People who are not in the army.

Conduit A channel or pipe that carries water.

Derelict Deserted and falling into ruins.

Excavate To remove earth and show hidden remains of the past such as buildings, graves, roads and ditches.

Exported Sent to another country.

Garrison Soldiers who guard a base or a fort.

Gaul An ancient region which in Roman times stretched from northern Italy to the Netherlands.

Germanic The name given to tribes who lived north of the Rhine and Danube frontiers of the Roman Empire.

Granary A building for storing grain.

Hoards Collections of valuable metals (coins or weapons) buried for safety.

Hypocaust The Roman heating system where hot air from a fire in the cellar passed under the floor and up flues in the walls.

Insulae Square blocks of buildings in a Roman town, formed by streets crossing at right angles.

Kilns Ovens for baking pottery and tiles.

Lavatory A place used for washing.

Mausoleums Buildings holding a tomb, usually with a room where offerings could be made to the dead person.

Milecastle A small fort, built at every Roman mile on Hadrian's Wall, holding a garrison of fifty troops.

Mortaria Mixing bowls with a rough surface for grinding foods.

Ramparts Banks of earth and stones usually used to protect villages or forts.

Toga A long piece of cloth which the Romans wrapped round themselves to make a loose robe.

Books to read

The Roman World by M Corbishley (Kingfisher, 1986)

Hadrian's Wall in the Days of the Romans by R Embleton & F Graham (Frank Graham, 1984)

The Roman Army by P Hodge (Longman, 1977)

Roman Britain by M O'Connell (Wayland, 1989)

Food and Cooking in Roman Britain by J Renfrew (English Heritage, 1985)

Roman Roads by P Warner (Wayland, 1980)

Growing up in Roman Britain by F Wilkins (Batsford, 1979)

Places to visit

Aldborough, North Yorkshire: town.
Baginton (The Lunt), West Midlands: reconstructed fort.
Bath, Avon: public baths and temple site.
Bignor, West Sussex: villa.
Carnarfon, Gwynedd: fort.
Canterbury, Kent: town house preserved under shopping precinct.
Fishbourne, West Sussex: palace.
Hadrian's Wall, Northumberland and Cumbria.
York: legionary fortress with preserved walls and towers.

Museums

Buxton, Derbyshire.
Canterbury, Kent.
Chester, Cheshire.
Cirencester, Gloucester.
Colchester, Essex.
Derby.
Dorchester, Dorset.
Hull, North Humberside.
Leicester.
Lincoln.
London: British Museum and Museum of London.
St Albans, Hertfordshire.
Winchester, Hampshire.
York.

Index

Picture acknowledgements

The publisher would like to thank the following for providing the pictures used in this book: Lesley and Roy Adkins 5, 12, 13, 18 (left), 19 (left), 28; Aerofilms 23; Dave Arthur 22 (top); Chester Museum 8; Michael Holford 6, 24 (left), 25 (bottom); Barry M. Marsden 11, 18 (right), 25 (top); Museum of London 20-21, 22 (bottom) 26, 27; Sheffield City Museum 24 (top); Unichrome (Bath) Ltd. 19 (right); Wayland Picture Library 14.

Artwork: Peter Bull 4, 9 (both), 10, 11, 14-15, 20-21, 28; Peter Dennis 7, 16-17, 23, 29 (left); Malcolm S. Walker cover, 29 (right)